BRIDAL STYLE

CONCISE EDITION

BRIDAL STYLE

CONCISE EDITION

NANCY DAVIS

HUGH LAUTER LEVIN ASSOCIATES, INC.

Copyright © 1997 Hugh Lauter Levin Associates, Inc.
Design by Ken Scaglia
Photo research by Leslie Conron Carola
and Kathy Farrell-Kingsley
ISBN 0-88363-597-6
Printed in China

❖ *(Title page) All the signs of a celebration: an elegant table setting, beautifully wrapped gifts, and, of course, fragrant flowers. Flowers by Elizabeth Ryan. Photo by Susan Wides.*

❖ *(Above) Magnolia leaves, gilded fern heads, and a single gardenia transform a simple box into a work of art—a suitable container for a gift for the bride. Flowers by Elizabeth Ryan. Photo by Z. Livnat.*

❖ *(Contents page) The bride's chair, decorated for the celebration with soft yellow roses and yards of pure white tulle, sets a romantic tone. Photo by Peter Högg.*

~ Contents ~

The W EDDING

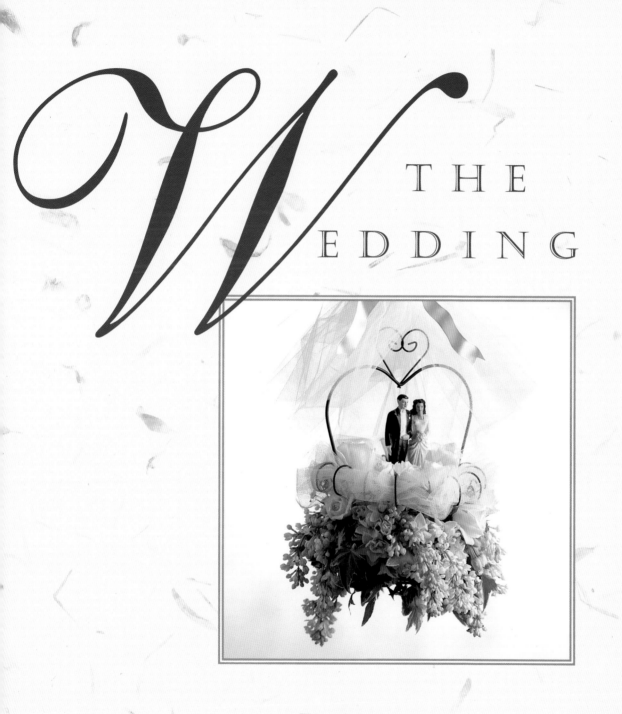

A wedding is the celebration of a lifetime, combining sweeping gestures, thoughtful details, and delicate touches. The way you choose to celebrate can reveal your interests, beliefs, attitudes, and hopes. For some brides and grooms, a wedding is a solemn ritual or a tender, private moment; for most, however, it is a meaningful and memorable day filled with joyous commotion.

Your wedding is a distinctive special event that you and your fiancé—through the countless choices you make about the ceremony, the reception, fashions, flowers, music, and food—can make uniquely your own.

Naturally, the ceremony itself is the most important part of the event, although frequently it is the briefest. Wedding planning tends to focus on the various celebrations surrounding the service—rehearsal dinners, receptions, or even breakfasts the morning after the wedding. They require the most planning—*and* are the scenes of the most revelry. It may be hard to believe how busy you will be with the seemingly endless decisions, meetings, and phone calls to arrange the details of your wedding. Will it take place in a church or a home or a garden? Will it be during the day or in the evening? Will you have a religious ceremony? Who will participate with you? How many guests will attend? Will you wear an antique ballgown or a modern sheath, a veil or hat or crown of flowers? Will you carry an all-white cascade of roses and lilies or a colorful nosegay of freshly picked favorites? Will your cake be chocolate or lemon or carrot? Will you dance to jazz or rock or country?

❖ *(Previous spread) Good marriages are made in heaven, they say. Carrying good wishes from on high, this bride-and-groom wedding cake topper floats earthward on a romantic cloud of tulle and fresh flowers. Photo by Peter Högg.*

❖ *(Opposite) The exquisite joy of the moment, radiating from this groom's face, is shared by the delighted guests. Photo by Christine Newman.*

❖ *(Right) A picture-perfect bride and her mother pause amid the festivities of a perfect summer wedding day. Photo by Mary Cooney for Pamela Benepe Photography.*

The key to all your wedding planning is organization: do a bit of reading, looking, comparing, and talk to your groom and family and friends about what is important to you. As the wedding approaches, try to complete each step on your list of preparations with calm and good humor. Remember that even if the minute-to-minute details of your wedding don't follow the course you've painstakingly set, there are very few mishaps that can mar the beauty of your special day.

～ THE RITUALS: ～ RELIGIOUS OR SECULAR?

Steeped in tradition and sacred to many, "holy matrimony" is a religious event that for many couples demands a religious service.

In the Roman Catholic church, marriage is one of seven sacraments. Because it is viewed as a very serious commitment, couples are generally required to complete premarital counseling in preparation for their life as husband and wife. A traditional Catholic wedding ceremony is frequently celebrated in conjunction with, or as part of, a special Nuptial Mass, although the mass itself is not required. The priest, the bride and groom, two witnesses, and an exchange of vows are the ingredients that are essential to a Catholic wedding ceremony.

In the Jewish tradition, marriage is also considered sacred, and although the ceremony may vary within the religion's Orthodox, Conservative, and Reform groups, the basic ritual is the same. The bride and groom stand under a *huppah*, or wedding canopy, during the service. Hebrew blessings are recited over wine that is shared by the couple; the bride then receives her wedding ring. The *ketubah*, or marriage contract, is read aloud, followed by the recitation of the Seven Blessings. The ceremony ends with the groom breaking a glass underfoot to symbolize the destruction of the Holy Temple in Jerusalem. This final act, in the happiest of moments, also serves to remind the couple that life can be very fragile.

With the exception of the Episcopal church, Protestant religions do not consider marriage a sacrament. It is, however, viewed as a holy union, with the ceremony based on passages from the Old and New Testaments. The service can be as short as ten minutes, or significantly longer, depending on the liturgy appropriate for certain denominations, or on the choices of the bride and groom. Whatever the duration, the basic ceremony contains three parts: the gathering words and opening prayers; the exchange of vows and rings; and the blessing of the couple and benediction.

Many wedding ceremonies share common rituals, regardless of religious or cultural differences. For instance, wine is part of many different ceremonies. An African-American wedding tradition of pouring a libation to invoke a blessing from the gods parallels the recitation of Hebrew blessings over wine at a Jewish service and the offering of wine to God at the Catholic Nuptial Mass or the Episcopalian service.

Another shared theme is the symbolic act of creating a union. Laotian couples are joined at the wrists by a "spiritual string"; a ritual cloth is used to wrap the wrists of the Ukrainian bride and groom; and at conventional Hindu weddings, the couple's hands are tied with a red thread and placed over a vessel that is filled with water, leaves, fruits, and flowers—what are considered to be the essentials of life. The fact that such traditions are still recognized today attests to the endurance of marriage as a social institution, rich in meaning.

❖ *At this Jewish service, the groom breaks a glass underfoot to symbolize the destruction of the Holy Temple of Jerusalem, a reminder of the fragility of life. Photo by Christine Newman.*

❖ *This contemporary wedding party, clearly free of the ancient custom that required attendants to dress like the bride in order to confuse the evil spirits, makes a sophisticated fashion statement. Photo by Barber Photography.*

All religions, from Judaism to Islam, Hinduism to Buddhism, and all the many divisions of Christianity—Roman Catholic, Eastern Orthodox, Baptist, Mormon, Methodist, Seventh Day Adventist, or Quaker, among many others—extol marriage as a joyous celebration. Ceremonies vary greatly in their content and symbolic gestures, but similar feelings—those of unity and devotion—will be present at any religious service you plan.

Not everyone, however, wants a storybook wedding, complete with a multitude of bridesmaids and elaborate preparations. For some, a civil ceremony or an intimate religious ceremony does the job. Personal choice or religious differences may dictate a civil service, and that is certainly as memorable and important a celebration as one with a cast of thousands.

Authorized officials who may perform civil ceremonies include judges, justices of the peace, county clerks, and mayors. Although a judge is likely to hold the service in his or her chambers, the ceremony could take place at almost any location you wish, providing the official agrees. The marriage license bureau in your area will provide you with a list of available officials.

～ TRADITIONS AND CUSTOMS ～

To some people, the familiar traditions and customs are simply silly superstitions. Others hold them as powerful rituals to be closely followed in order to assure a happy union. Whatever personal significance they may hold, wedding traditions have obscure, sometimes mystical histories that only add to their popularity.

Many of today's traditions originated in ancient Greece and Rome. They are highly symbolic and largely deal with fertility, sexuality, and good old-fashioned magic.

The custom of the bride wearing "something old, something new, something borrowed, something blue," for example, is taken from an old English rhyme. Interpretations may vary, but, generally, "old" and "borrowed" are thought to honor past traditions; a "new" item will hopefully bring luck in the future; and "blue" has been a symbol of fidelity and modesty, as it was in ancient Israel where it was customary for brides to trim their wedding robes with blue ribbons.

Food has its place among the honored traditions as well. Rice, a symbol of fertility, is often thrown at the couple as they leave their ceremony, although, now, more environmentally conscious wedding guests toss birdseed or rose petals. The gesture of throwing something on the bride and groom is a metaphor for showering them with the good things of life. In Asia, the use of rice signifies a "full pantry." Following Italian and Greek

❖ *Hand in hand, a joyous bride and groom exit the church amid a blizzard of good wishes, in the form of confetti, showered on them by their family and friends. Photo by Richard Fanning.*

customs, the almond, once a symbol of undying love and youth, is still sugarcoated and given as reception favors to wedding guests.

The lore surrounding wedding traditions is not always romantic. For instance, engagement rings originally indicated that the groom-to-be had basically purchased his fiancée; the woman was seen to be his exclusive property by virtue of wearing his ring. And, once the wedding ceremony took place, the same ring served as the wedding band. It was in the eighth century that the giving of an engagement token was first recorded: a Jewish groom gave his bride-to-be a coin to show that he was financially secure.

Not surprisingly it was the French who first associated the ring with love. In sixteenth- and seventeenth-century Europe, gimmal rings were popular signs of engagement. This type of ring with joined or interlocked parts could be divided in two—one half worn by the woman, the other half by the man. Later, the separate rings could be joined and worn together by the woman as her wedding ring.

The diamond engagement ring often associated with today's betrothals did not fully come into fashion until the mid-nineteenth century, when the South African diamond mines opened. Before that, diamonds had been far too scarce and expensive. The

❖ *Mother Nature could not have been more cooperative this day. The sunset on a Nantucket beach offers a tranquil, unforgettable reception setting for these newlyweds and a close circle of friends. Photo by Lane du Pont.*

year 1477, however, marks the first time a woman was the lucky recipient of an engagement ring with a precious jewel as part of its design. The famous story relates that Archduke Maximilian of Austria was so busy making war that he presented Mary of Burgundy with a diamond ring already in his possession—he simply did not have time to find anything else. Until that time in European society, women had not been permitted to wear rings that contained gems.

The perfectly circular shape of the wedding band itself has long been a symbol of endless love. Early records note that the rings worn by the ancient Egyptians were made of iron, steel, brass, copper, silver, and gold, as well as of less durable materials such as leather and rush. Then, the band was placed on the third finger of the left hand, as it is today. The ancients believed that one vein ran from that finger straight to the heart.

❖ *Icons for the unending love wished for the bride and groom—gold wedding rings for both. Photo by Peter Hogg.*

Surprisingly, evil spirits have played a major role in the development of many wedding traditions. In the days of ancient Rome, unseen tricksters were thought to lurk about, posing a threat to the bride and groom. The current practice of inviting men and women to be members of the wedding party evolved from one old Roman custom that required the presence of ten witnesses at a marriage ceremony in order to outsmart jealous demons. The bride's attendants dressed in clothes similar to her own, and the same was true of the groom and his ushers. It was hoped that the spirits waiting to rob the couple of their happiness would be confused by the similar clothing and would be thwarted in their attempt to carry out their wicked plans. To further thwart the spirits, the Romans performed the chivalrous act of carrying the bride safely across the threshold to prevent the jealous spirits from tripping her and spoiling her joy.

The earliest grooms practiced marriage by capture. A bride was "stolen" and taken into hiding until family and friends called off their search for her. The term *honeymoon* has its origins in the period that followed the "capture." For thirty days (or one full moon), the newlyweds drank mead, a brew made by the ancient Gauls and Anglo-Saxons from fermented honey and water. Mead, which is still used in Ireland to toast newlyweds as they depart for their honeymoon, was said to have powers of virility and fertility.

The custom of having a "best man" is believed to date back to wedding captures as well. A friend of the groom was needed to fight off and stall the bride's family while the couple made an escape.

The garter toss, another wedding custom, has its roots in an old British ritual called "flinging the stocking." After the wedding, guests would storm the bridal chamber and snatch the couple's stockings, which the guests then took turns flinging at the newlyweds' faces. The first guest whose stocking touched the bride's or groom's nose would be the next to marry. Today, the bride's bouquet toss continues that custom: it is thought that the single woman who catches the bouquet will marry soon.

Tying cans and shoes to the newlyweds' car remains a popular prank carried out by friends and family. The noise of these items dragging along is meant to chase away evil spirits. In an early Anglo-Saxon ritual, the bride presented the groom with one of her slippers, which he then hung over their bed. This act symbolized the transfer of responsibility for the bride from her father to her new husband.

❖ *Styles in shades of rich white—all the way down to the littlest bridesmaid—dress a sizable bridal party. Photo by Barber Photography.*

~ ETHNIC AND ~
CULTURAL INFLUENCES

The impact that families and forebears still have on American weddings is proof of strong emotional ties to individual heritages. Ethnic practices, religious or social, are continually woven into ceremonies by new generations who choose to honor the old.

The myriad of interesting ethnic customs still observed lend great insight into the diverse practices of foreign lands. Many are joyful, some seem sad, but all are important threads that reveal a rich tapestry of tradition.

❖ *(Left) The African-based symbols embroidered in gold on these wedding garments are exquisite reminders of a cultural tradition embraced by this stunning couple. Photo courtesy of Darryl and Kerri Washington.*

❖ *(Above) Luxurious silks wrap this couple in traditional Japanese garments seen here joining hands to share the Western tradition of cutting their wedding cake. Photo by Barber Photography.*

❖ *(Opposite) This just-married couple basks in a cocoon of diaphanous wedding veil and setting sun. Photo by Barber Photography.*

THE DRESS

*F*rom the first step down the aisle to the very last dance, the vision of the bride captivates all who witness the wedding celebration. That electrifying first sight of the bride in her finery is what remains in the minds of the guests. It is a lasting image that reflects the beauty and romance of the occasion.

Because your gown is likely to be the most elaborate and luxurious article of clothing you ever purchase, you will want to consider all the options available. Whether you choose to wear an elaborate gown, an elegant suit, a simple dress, or an outfit of sentimental value, the clothes you wear should make you happy and reflect your personal style. To help you sort through the possibilities, here are some things to keep in mind as you shop.

To begin, it is best to be a bit cautious about where you buy your wedding gown. Unless you are wearing an heirloom, having your gown custom-made, or making it yourself, you'll be visiting one or more bridal retail stores. A reliable, full-service bridal salon will assist you in every step, from discussing current bridal styles to overseeing your own final fitting. You will be paying for quality and expertise—and perhaps peace of mind. Buying from a bargain resource could leave much to chance when purchasing such a supremely important item. Of course, a reliable dressmaker can handle the alterations, if necessary.

It is important to realize that most bridal gowns commonly arrive twelve weeks after they have been ordered. While some

❖ *(Previous spread) Cascading panels of ivory Alençon lace surround the skirt and chapel train of this white silk shantung gown. More lovely lace shapes the sleeves and trims the bodice. Gown by Jim Hjelm.*

❖ *(Opposite) The graceful lines of this elegant shoulder-baring gown are accented by fabric rosettes trimming the waist. Photo by Barber Photography.*

❖ *(Right) Less is more: The classic headband is an elegant understatement when combined with the spectacular lines of organza bustle, cabbage roses, and cathedral train on this quiet, refined gown. Gown by Carolina Herrera.*

manufacturers take longer, others may deliver in eight to ten weeks. In either case, it's wise to keep the twelve-week mark in mind once your date is set.

Since every detail of your wedding gown reflects your personal style, it is best to consider in depth all of the possible variations in color, fabric, silhouette, skirt length, sleeves, and neckline. The following definitions of clothing design terms will give you a clearer understanding of your choices.

White still reigns as the favored color for a gown, with variations of cream and off-white shades ranking next in popularity. Satin, silk, organza, organdy, taffeta, velvet, chiffon, lace, cotton, linen, tulle, and rich brocades are just some of the fabrics that you may touch during the search for your gown. Some dresses simply rely on the beauty of the fabric and the lines of the gown to make a statement. Others may be trimmed with a sprinkling of sequins, beads, pearls, or crystals. Scrolls of embroidered passementerie (a fancy edging or trimming made of braid, cord, beading, or metallic thread), fabric flowers, satin cording, rich ribbons, or bows may also be used.

The Line

❖ *Empire silhouette* refers to a dress style with a high waistline that starts just under the bustline and is usually defined by a seam.

❖ *Princess line* refers to a classic silhouette that is shaped with vertical seams. It fits snugly through the rib cage, has a seamless waist, then flares slightly to the hem.

❖ A *sheath* is a straight, body-hugging gown, often floor-length; it is sometimes designed with a train that may or may not detach.

❖ A *strapless gown* is designed to bare the shoulders. This elegant style is often topped with a coordinating jacket.

❖ *(Opposite) Shadow and light: Passementerie details heighten the drama of this sumptuous wedding dress. Photo by Barber Photography.*
❖ *(Right) A slim column of lace creates an elegant bridal sheath with a wedding band collar. Photo by Richard Fanning.*

≈ 25 ≈

The Skirt

❖ A *bouffant skirt* is a very full skirt, gathered at the waist, and usually worn over a crinoline.

❖ A *ballgown skirt* is a style designed with a natural waistline and a very full, flared skirt.

❖ An *intermission-length skirt*, which is also called a hi-lo skirt, falls midcalf in front, then extends to the floor in back.

❖ A *tiered skirt* has a series of layers or flounces that fall in graduated rows.

The Train

❖ A *bustle* is a skirt with a gathering of fabric, ruffles, or other design details that fill out the back of the gown.

❖ A *train* is formed by fabric that is either part of the skirt or detachable and that trails in back of the gown.

❖ A *sweep train* is a short train that "sweeps" the floor.

❖ A *chapel train* is one that extends one and a third yards from the waist.

❖ A *cathedral train* is one that extends three yards from the waist.

The Sleeve

❖ A *cap sleeve* is a short, fitted sleeve that just barely covers the shoulders.

❖ A *cape sleeve* is a sleeve achieved by placing a circular piece of fabric over each shoulder and then stitching it to the bodice, giving a caped effect over each arm.

❖ *Poufed sleeves* are very full at the top, and can be long or short.

❖ A *fitted-point sleeve* is a long sleeve that falls just below the wrist, descending to a point.

❖ A *Juliet sleeve* is a long sleeve poufed at the shoulder but fitted on the forearm.

❖ A *petal sleeve* is a short sleeve made of overlapping panels that are curved at the hem, creating a petal-shaped effect.

❖ *This satin gown has scalloped edges on a fitted bodice that leads to a deep V-back. A row of pretty bows lines the skirt and its sweeping train. Designer: Michele Vincent/Alfred Angelo.*

The Waistline

❖ A *natural waistline* is a waist with a seam at the narrowest part of the midriff—at the point of the natural waistline.

❖ A *basque waistline* is an elongated waist that dips to a V-shaped point at the center of the front of the dress.

❖ A *dropped waistline* is a waist with a slightly gathered seam line several inches below the natural waistline.

The Neckline

❖ An *illusion yoke* has transparent lace or netting fitted at the neckline and shoulders, often extending down to the bustline.

❖ An *on- or off-the-shoulder neckline* is one that can be worn up on the shoulders or down.

❖ A *jewel neckline* is rounded to follow the natural contours of the neck, creating a simple background for jewels.

❖ A *wedding band collar* is a traditional stand-up band that circles the neck.

❖ A *sabrina neckline* is a straight neckline beginning two inches inside of the shoulder edge.

❖ A *sweetheart neckline* is a moderately low neckline that begins two inches from the shoulder edge and has a heart-shaped center front.

❖ A *portrait collar* is a neckline fabric that frames the shoulders, often gathered in the center above the bustline with a decorative fabric detail or ornament.

❖ A *scoop neck* is a low, curved neckline cut deep in the front, back, or both.

❖ A *U-back* is a plunging, U-shaped scoop design on the back of a gown.

❖ *(Above)} On a cloud: Diaphanous tiers of ribbon-hemmed tulle were used for the delicate skirt, train, and veil. Photo by Harold Hechler Associates.*

❖ *(Right) Traditional bridal lines are treated to embroidery and a feminine bustled back. Gown by Christian Dior Bridal Collection.*

~ A HEADPIECE AND VEIL ~

Like most fashion elements, headpieces range from classic to contemporary, with many modifications along the way. While actually experimenting with choices at the shop is the best way to determine the right style, there is one guideline that usually applies: simpler headpieces generally complement more dramatic dresses, while more detailed ones may work well with classic, understated looks.

The style you choose should complement your gown, flatter your face, and be comfortable enough to wear from ceremony through reception. The basic types of headpieces are all subject to a variety of trims, so that each may be unique. In addition to a tiara, which resembles a crown, other choices include a headband, comb, picture hat, Juliet cap, mantilla, wreath, snood, or fresh flowers.

"There's a cleaner, more sophisticated look popular now," says headpiece designer Tia Mazza, owner of Tia Mazza Millinery in Manhattan. "Styles are simpler and not as fussy as many in the past. I do a great deal of handwork and make lots of small, delicate tiaras, elegant pillboxes, and headbands."

Veils come in a variety of lengths and can be secured to the headpiece. Elaborate veils are often detachable so they

❖ *(Left) A pearl-studded tulle veil with porcelina roses, white lilac, and still-green acacia is the bride's crowning glory. Flowers by Karen Frerichs. Photo by Peter Högg.*

❖ *(Opposite) The simple elbow-length veil and uncomplicated headpiece provide appropriate contrast to the exquisite beaded lace details of this Italian satin gown with princess shaping and rolled satin rosettes at the back waist. Gown by Jim Hjelm.*

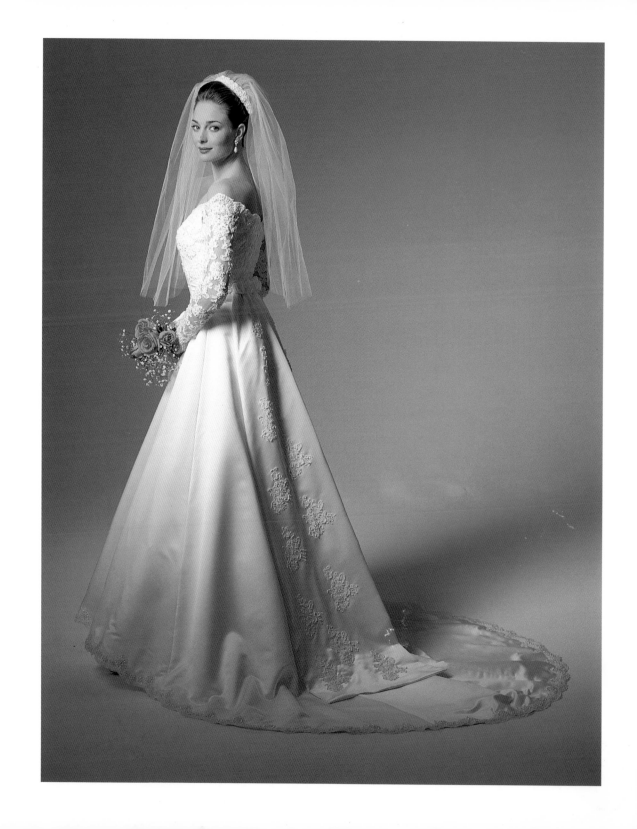

❖ *(Above, clockwise from bottom left) Folds of silk trimmed with tiny pearl clusters create a back comb with understated elegance. Designer: Michele Piccione for Alfred Angelo Dream Maker; A side comb of roses and beads adds a soft accent. Designer: Michele Piccione for Alfred Angelo Dream Maker; Pearl-kissed illusion, tucked into a sleek back bun, falls gracefully over the shoulders. Designer: Michele Piccione for Alfred Angelo Dream Maker; A tuft of airy tulle falls from a cluster of fresh, fragrant roses. Photo courtesy of Wildflower.*

can be removed for the reception. Mazza's most popular veils are the *blusher* (an elbow-length veil placed over the bride's face to be lifted during the ceremony); *fingertip* (brushes the tips of the fingers); *cathedral* (very formal, three yards in length); and, very recently, the *butterfly* (a folded-over circle of tulle). Other frequently chosen lengths include the *birdcage* (ends just below the chin); *flyaway* (brushes the shoulders); and *ballet* or *waltz* (extends to the knee). And for the most formal gowns, veils that trail behind the bride are also available in several lengths.

On your wedding day, adornment can seem an art with accessories that are packed with pure style. Naturally, the selection of your gown comes first, but the shoes, gloves, purse, and jewelry you wear with it can be every bit as important.

❖ *A perfect marriage: Fresh lilacs create the headpiece for this simple veil covering the bride's face and head. The natural lines of the dress echo the natural form of the flowers. Photo by Marili Forastieri.*

~ SHOES ~

Ask any bride who has stood, danced, and greeted her way through her wedding day what you should know about shoes, and her first word will most certainly be *comfort*.

A word to the wise: Try not to make a drastic change from the heel height you're accustomed to. If you can generally be found in flats, chances are that a high heel may spoil some of your fun. Should you decide to wear a different heel, make sure the shoe fits well in every way.

Your choice of footwear also needs to be practical depending on the type of celebration you've planned. For instance, if you are having an outdoor ceremony or reception, you would find it difficult to walk on grass wearing heels. It is also best to buy your shoes soon after you've bought a gown: that way, you'll have plenty of time to break them in around the house, and to wear them at scheduled dress fittings.

Of all the elements that make up the bridal outfit, wedding shoes are the one purchase that brides are able to wear again.

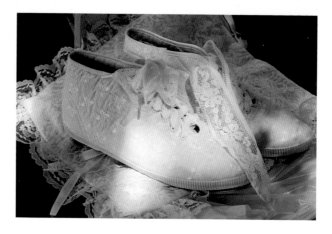

❖ *(Above) Step out and have fun: If you can't imagine wearing anything but high heels for the ceremony, consider a second pair of shoes—wedding sneakers—just for the reception. Photo by Georgia Sheron.*

❖ *(Opposite) The strong, dramatic lines of this sculptural, intricately beaded bodice is balanced by a cloudlike billowing skirt and veil. Photo by Barber Photography.*

~ GLOVES ~

The etiquette of gloves was once dicated by the formality of the wedding, time of the ceremony, and style of the gown. Now, your gown's sleeve length seems to be the only determining factor. "We offer four basic lengths for brides," says designer Reem Acra of Reem Bridals in New York City, whose stretch cotton gloves are entirely handmade. "The *wrist glove* goes with all sleeves; the *tea-length* reaches midway between wrist and elbow and looks good with most sleeves; the *elbow-length* (which extends just past the elbow) is popular with off-the-shoulder styles; and the longest gloves, *opera-length*, go beautifully with sleeveless or strapless gowns."

When you pose for photographs or walk down the aisle, gloves can lend a graceful accent, but you may be concerned about what to do once you reach the altar. La Crasia, owner of La Crasia Gloves, Inc., in New York City, explains: "The gloves must be removed during the ceremony for the wedding ring, unless the bride has chosen a very fine crochet over which the ring can be placed. But we've designed kidskin gloves with the stitching removed from the ring finger; the leather is then folded into the glove during the exchange of rings and later stitched back on at our showroom."

～ JEWELS ～

The jewelry you wear on your wedding day may be decided by the formality of your ceremony and reception, the lines of your gown, or even the style of your hair. You may already own some lovely pieces or receive a wedding day gift from your groom or be given an heirloom with special meaning.

Pearls are the lustrous gems that most often come to mind when it's time to choose wedding day jewels. Whether a simple strand for a portrait collar, or earrings set with rhinestones, pearls often make the perfect statement. They are both romantic and traditional and, since ancient times, have been treasured as symbols of purity and modesty.

Whatever your personal choices, Claire Kellam, executive vice president of Christian Dior Jewelry, notes that in addition to classic gold, many of today's brides are considering white metals such as platinum for their wedding rings and jewelry. Kellam recommends that brides follow these guidelines when making their decisions:

❖ *(Opposite) This bride is beautifully dressed all the way down to long satiny gloves. Photo by Sarah Merians.*
❖ *(Above) Softly scrunched tea-length satin gloves add the perfect finishing touch to this short pearl-and-sequin-studded, all-over lace sheath. Designer: Michele Vincent/Alfred Angelo.*

❖ If your dress has an elaborately detailed bodice, you may want to forego a necklace and focus instead on earrings. The more detailed the dress, the simpler the earrings, and vice versa.

❖ When choosing earrings, keep stature and scale in mind. If you are petite, choose more delicate looks, such as drop pearls. Taller women can carry bigger styles, such as a large, single pearl or a dramatic pearl cluster.

❖ A simple bodice often calls for a necklace. Certainly, a strapless or off-the-shoulder gown requires something around the neck—perhaps a double-strand pearl choker.

❖ If your dress is strapless or has short sleeves, you may want to wear a bracelet. Consider a single- or double-strand pearl design.

❖ Where your bridesmaids are concerned, a gift of jewelry can accomplish several things: it may serve as a beautiful memento and also lend a uniform look to the wedding party—if that's something you desire.

❖ *(Top, right) Careful consideration should be given to wedding day accessories, particularly jewels. Here, a fabulous faux pearl necklace and drop earrings add a dramatic touch. Photo by Marili Forastieri.*

❖ *(Right) This elaborate bodice and high neck makes the choice of jewelry simple— none is needed. Dress by Jessica McClintock. Photo by Tim Geany.*

❖ *(Opposite) A strong neckline and sparkling beads adorning the bodice of this pretty gown make jewelry other than delicate drop earrings unnecessary. Designer: Michele Vincent/Alfred Angelo.*

❖ (Opposite) Sheer, sophisticated point d'esprit covers a gown styled with a silk crepe halter bodice, basque waist, and sweep train. Gown by Carolina Herrera.

❖ (Above) The soft petals and beads trimming this bride's tulle gown seem to reflect the beautiful garden setting. Photo by Marili Forastieri.

❖ (Right) There's a most regal feeling to this elegant bridal gown by Carolina Herrera, with its high neck, fitted bodice, and long, graceful sleeves. Photo courtesy of Sean Psomas, Wildflower.

❖ *(Left) Harlequin embroidery highlights a classically sleek Duchess satin gown with a petal skirt and illusion train. Gown by Carolina Herrera.*

❖ *(Opposite) Understated elegance, all in white: This bride and her attendants compose a striking wedding party in stunning sheaths. Photo by Barber Photography.*

THE CEREMONY

*W*hether it begins with a march down a church aisle, a cab ride to City Hall, a walk into a trellised garden, or a descent down your own staircase, a marriage ceremony will unite you and the person you love as husband and wife. Regardless of the setting you select, this event is a universal rite that signifies the beginning of a new life together.

The religious or civil service that you choose will establish the basic format of your wedding ceremony. Those elements that make a wedding ceremony unique, however, arise from the thoughts and emotions you and your groom choose to share with each other and with your guests and the ways you express these sentiments.

Writing part or all of your ceremony is one way to express your feelings. Personalized vows that reflect your commitment to each other must come from the heart, and your own words can reaffirm the themes of love, joy, fidelity, and respect that are so meaningful. As you prepare your vows, though, be sure to consult first with the officiant performing your service to determine which, if any, passages may be mandatory.

You may want to have printed wedding programs that include important elements of your ceremony. As a keepsake as well as a guide, these programs can enhance the wedding for your guests by allowing them to follow the service more closely. The program may hold a note of thanks to parents, a description of a unique tradition, a prayer or quotation or poem, or a tribute to a deceased relative or friend. Standard information in a wedding program usually

❖ *(Previous spread) Under a canopy of softly lit ficus trees, this bride and groom exchange vows in a Jewish ceremony. Photo by Christine Newman.*

❖ *(Opposite) A brilliant sunset—and dozens of guests—await the arrival of the bride and groom at this dramatic outdoor pavilion setting. Photo by Barber Photography.*

❖ *(Right) A formal wedding ceremony in a Catholic church is replete with ritual and sacred symbols. Photo by Harold Hechler Associates.*

includes the wedding date, location, and time; the names of those in the wedding party; the officiant or co-celebrants; and any musicians or soloists and the titles of the music performed.

The music you select for your wedding will set the tone for your ceremony from the prelude through the final joyous recessional. Whether you're planning to be married in a majestic church or at home or in a more unusual setting, choose music that is appropriate to your wedding environment.

The grandeur of a trumpet flourish, the classic dignity of a church organ, or the charming simplicity of a soloist or string quartet—decide who will perform your wedding music, and surround yourself and your guests with the sounds you love. You may want

❖ (Left) In keeping with tradition, this Russian Orthodox couple stands while jeweled crowns are held above their heads. Photo by Christine Newman.

❖ (Opposite) Gracefully acknowledging the poignancy of the moment, this groom, waiting at the altar, accepts the hand of his bride from her father. Photo by John M. Cerritelli, Prestige-Barkley.

to stay with the traditional—Lohengrin's "Bridal Chorus" and Mendelssohn's "Wedding March"—or possibly something lighter or more intimate. Love songs and ballads, even folk songs and movie themes, might be among your list of favorites. Your organist or a musical friend or family member can give you some suggestions, but be sure to clear your final choices with the officiant who will perform the ceremony.

～ THE WAYS WE WED ～

A wedding offers you and your fiancé the perfect opportunity to express yourselves, whether by incorporating a favorite interest or an unusual experience as a theme. For many couples, the object is to create an unforgettable day—in more ways than one.

Some couples have unique ways of tying the knot. When two New York City floral designers decided to marry, they had no way of knowing that the city's biggest blizzard in decades would hit on the same day as their wedding. Naturally, they worried about whether their family, friends, and officiant would arrive not just on time, but at all. Somehow nearly every guest *and* the officiant defied the odds and made it to the loft high above the city that the couple had chosen for their ceremony and reception. With the storm raging outside, the lushly decorated interior space looked especially romantic in contrast.

What do two floral designers choose for their wedding decor? Tons of lilacs, verbinium, French tulips, Anna roses from the south of France, lisianthus, and daffodils. The groom is from Holland, and his father and stepmother are also florists there. They did almost everything. Pink and red rose petals lined window ledges, bouquets with wired ribbons were carried on each service tray, blooming pear

branches were placed on the floor around pedestals that held even more flowers. No two arrangements were alike; they were positioned on the floor all around the loft in different types of urns. The colors were very pale and cool: lavender, blues, soft yellow, blush pink, and a range of greens from light to dark all created this incredible environment. An entire spring garden was brought inside on a wildly snowy day.

Many of today's couples choose to marry far away from home, and no locale is more coveted than tropical Hawaii. Alicia Bay Laurel, the director of A Wedding Made in Paradise, based on the island of Maui, has coordinated hundreds of long-distance weddings for couples who seek the unusual and can't be there to plan the event.

"Some months I'll have as many as thirty weddings to work on," says Laurel, who regularly gets calls and letters from nearly every country — Singapore to Scotland. "I've planned a Jewish wedding for an Argentinian and Canadian couple, a ceremony for a Danish architect and his Chinese bride complete with canoe transportation, and an off-shore catamaran service officiated by a Samoan minister. But one of my favorites was the wedding on horseback of two grandparents — their grandchildren urged the union. The bride raised thoroughbreds and the

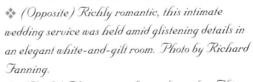

❖ (Opposite) Richly romantic, this intimate wedding service was held amid glistening details in an elegant white-and-gilt room. Photo by Richard Fanning.

❖ (Right) Marriage with a modern edge: This Christian ceremony took place in a spare, sophisticated setting dressed with dramatic floral arrangements. Photo by Harold Hechler Associates.

groom was a horseshoer, so the mode of transportation was a logical one. The ceremony was performed high on a hillside overlooking the ocean. It just took your breath away."

For Sharmila Anandasabapathy and Andrew Sikora, their marriage joined two cultures as well as two lives. Born in Sri Lanka, Sharmila moved with her family to New York when she was only an infant. When she and her American-born fiancé became engaged, they talked of having a simple civil ceremony. However, the service, held at the home of the bride's parents, happily evolved into one that represented both families' beliefs. First, a judge married the couple in a traditional ceremony. Sharmila wore a white sari and Andrew wore a tuxedo. This was followed by a blessing from a Catholic priest, in keeping with the Sikoras' religion.

Then a Vedic ceremony, an Indian ritual with a cultural rather than religious emphasis, was performed by an Indian doctor. For this service, Andrew wore a Nehru-style tunic and pants. Sharmila changed into a traditional red sari (red symbolizing the dawn, considered to be the beginning of life). The sari was patterned with a grapevine motif borrowed from the one worn by the bride's great-grandmother.

❖ (Opposite) Soaring timber beams warm the interior of this stunning stone chapel. The magic of the celebration below adds its own special warmth. Photo by Richard Fanning.

❖ (Right) The Manhattan loft chosen by two floral designers for their own marriage featured exquisite flowers and handmade papier-mache chandeliers crafted for the occasion by one of their groomsmen. Photo courtesy of Bentley Meeker Lighting and Staging Inc., N.Y.

❖ (Top, left) This Sri Lankan bride, raised in America, planned a dual ceremony with her groom. Here, she walks down the aisle on her father's arm dressed in a white westernized gown for a civil service. Photo by J. Gerard Smith.

❖ (Left) For the Hindu ceremony, her American groom escorts a young best man, both dressed in traditional Sri Lankan garments. Photo by J. Gerard Smith.

❖ (Above) The bride appears in the symbolic red sari she wore for the Hindu marriage ceremony. Photo by David Lindner.

As part of the Vedic ceremony, the bride and groom exchange floral garlands. Since they are worn close to the chest, this act is symbolically seen as an exchange of hearts. The groom then expresses his love and commitment by tying a *Thali,* or gold necklace, around the bride's neck. A highlight of the ceremony followed next, when Sharmila and Andrew performed the *Supta padi,* or "seven steps," as a symbol of their life together. Before each step they took, the couple recited the ceremony's verses. "We take the first step, a step toward plenty," it begins. Steps toward "energy and strength; virtues, the inner wealth; lifelong friendship; the welfare of our families; health in all seasons; and happiness born of wisdom" followed in order. "The combination of the two different ceremonies made both of our families happy," says Sharmila, "and everyone had to give a little bit. Our friends also found it really interesting."

The wedding rite means something different to every couple who takes part in it. If you rely on your own creative ideas and the resources to accommodate them, few dreams need go unfulfilled.

❖ *When only a kiss will do. Photos by Laurie Klein.*

❖ (Above) Garlands of Osiana roses, champagne roses, and French
tulips, with flanking candelabra, transform this white marble fireplace
into a suitable backdrop for the exchange of wedding vows. Flowers by
Sylvia Tidwell. Photo by Grey Crawford.

❖ (Opposite) For a spectacular ceremony with everything draped in
white, tiny star-like white ceiling lights add a celestial touch. Photo by
Greg Hark.

❖ (Above) In the most serious of moments, a little laughter helps ease the tension. This bride may have forgotten her lines, but she inspires giggles all around. Photo by Phyllis L. Keenan.

❖ (Above, right) Two officiants took part in this wedding ceremony between a bride and groom of different religions. Photo by John M. Cerritelli, Prestige-Barkley.

❖ (Opposite) Top, left: The structure of this magnificent towering temple is matched in size and drama by the floral huppah created for this Jewish wedding ceremony. Bottom, left: A splendid Spanish-Portuguese temple in New York City is the site for this moving ceremony. Right: For a service set in a hotel ballroom, richly draped fabric creates a huppah with elegant lines. Photos by Harold Hechler Associates.

❖ (Left) A cliffside setting in upstate New York offers a breathtaking view—and wedding picture—for this newlywed couple. Photo by Richard Fanning.

❖ (Opposite) With the sun setting on nearby hills and the ocean before them, this couple exchange their wedding vows. Photo by Barber Photography.

❖ (Above) Joyous ritual: This happy bride signs the ketubah, or
marriage contract, in the presence of a rabbi and her husband.
Photo by Richard Fanning.

❖ (Opposite) Let the ceremony begin: The groom and his best man look
for the bride to begin her walk down a beautiful country aisle. Photo by
Barber Photography.

❖ (Above) One little flower girl and then another have their turns
at a very grown-up moment: a touch of lipstick for the wedding day.
The ring bearer suddenly feels bashful in the presence of the beautiful
bride. Photos by Barber Photography. And a flower girl wearing a
pretty wreath chats shyly with the bride. Photo by Maureen DeFries.
❖ (Opposite) A beaming bride and father begin their procession.
Photo by Barber Photography.

❖ *(Opposite) Dozens of white balloons head for the heavens as this bride and groom are pronounced married. Photo by Barber Photography.*
❖ *(Above) A stolen moment for the bride and groom to share a private toast before the public celebration starts. Photo by Barber Photography.*

THE FLOWERS

The beauty and symbolism of flowers lend a special meaning to many of the most important occasions in our lives. A fragrant bouquet or a colorful, carefully crafted arrangement of the freshest blossoms enhances any decoration scheme. Naturally, when it comes to your wedding celebration, the flowers you choose require careful consideration.

In order to create a design, a florist needs to know certain facts about your wedding day: the ceremony and reception sites, the times of day, the style of your gown, and the color of your bridesmaids' dresses (it may help to have fabric swatches) are all essential elements to be considered. It is only natural to want your wedding festivities to be visually harmonious. Remember, though, this is *your* wedding, *your* day, so don't be afraid to express your own wishes, and to indicate to the florist how much or how little help you feel you need. Bring your florist to visit the ceremony and reception sites so that he or she can have a clear idea of what you envision. View the albums of past work and ask for suggestions and estimates within your budget. A true professional will take the time to understand your wishes and try to fulfill them.

Most floral designers agree that a bride should arrive for a first meeting armed with lots of tear sheets from magazines showing examples of flowers she likes *and* dislikes.

❖ *(Previous spread) Sprigs of pine boughs punctuate a standard of soft pastel-colored roses arranged for an elegant wedding. Flowers by Elizabeth Ryan. Photo by Z. Lionat.*

❖ *(Opposite) A sumptuous topiary centerpiece in white and soft pastels makes a lush addition to reception tables. Flowers by Paul Bott. Photo by Bill Margerin.*

❖ *(Right) Porcelina roses, lisanthus, hydrangea, and Queen Anne's lace festoon a tall candelabra, creating the scene for a fabulous wedding centerpiece. Flowers by Elizabeth Ryan. Photo by Z. Lionat.*

Tear sheets and photos help guide the florist to your specific tastes and the direction your wedding look will take.

Be sure to mention any flowers that have special meaning for you and your fiancé. If there was ever a time to surround yourselves with a favorite fragrance, color, and design, this is it. Some floral designers also suggest that you compose a list of appropriate adjectives describing what you would like to convey through the display flowers, even if you are not sure of the specific names of the blossoms. Such phrases as stark, linear, and clean; lush, full, and natural; colorful, fun, and happy; or romantic, soft, and light can often be more revealing than pictures.

Naturally your wishes are of primary importance, but there are two factors that help determine which flowers you might include in your wedding decorations. The first is the time of year you plan to marry. Most florists will advise that choosing seasonal flowers is wise. Not only does it make good economic sense (specially grown, imported flowers can be more expensive), but many brides prefer that the flowers decorating their wedding be representative of their region as well as the climate.

Although the rose, splendid in all its forms, remains the most popular of all wedding flowers throughout the year, there are dozens of other ideal seasonal choices. For spring celebrations, a beautiful selection of blooms may include bulbs (try tulips, anemones, ranunculus, and daffodils); sweet blossoms (peach, cherry, and apple); and an assortment of pussy willows, forsythia, heather, waxflowers, and roses. For summer through fall, some favorites are lilies, stephanotis, monte casino, and the many varieties of carnations. In the winter, many brides ask for all white flowers, such as roses, stephanotis, carnations, orchids, and gardenias—often with a touch of fragrant evergreens.

❖ *(Previous spread) A rose globe topiary and a runner of Jacaranda and Champagne roses laced with ivy and gilded lemon leaves grace the head table at this elegant wedding. Flowers by Sylvia Tidwell. Photo by Grey Crawford.*

❖ *(Left) Color explodes in a fragrant arrangement of lilies, roses, anemones, and Queen Anne's lace that creates a dramatic ambiance for a formal setting. Flowers by Fabrice. Photo by Z. Livnat.*

The second major factor that affects your floral scheme is the formality of your wedding. An outdoor celebration may call for bouquets and centerpieces with a "just-picked" look inspired by summer fields. But for a black tie event held in a hotel, you might want a more tailored view, perhaps flowers of all one color—crimson or lavender—set beside candelabras. However, don't hesitate to have what others might consider informal flowers at your formal celebration. Your first criteria should always be those blooms, or boughs, that reflect your vision and make you happy.

～ THE BOUQUET ～

Fresh flowers can enhance any chosen setting for either the ceremony or reception, but it is your bridal bouquet that often makes the most lasting impression. When it comes to choosing a shape, your florist may create any number of pleasing designs. There are three styles that remain most popular: the flowing *cascade bouquet*, the classic *nosegay*, and the graceful *arm bouquet*. Because each of these basic styles can, of course, be styled and modified to your liking, be sure to discuss your preferences with your floral designer.

Buttercups, lilacs, and lilies of the valley; roses, ranunculus, and bachelor's buttons; stephanotis, sweet peas, and forsythia—the limitless colors, combinations, and heady fragrances are easily translated into unforgettable arrangements by a floral designer. Your idea may be to create rich contrasts and dramatic shapes or delicate shades worked into neat nosegays. Together you and the florist can design a beautiful bouquet.

❖ *White on white: A delicate bouquet of stephanotis poised on lustrous white damask creates visual impact and says just as much about color as a vibrant colored bouquet. Flowers and photo courtesy of Wildflower.*

Since color can be incorporated into any aspect of floral decorations many brides choose white only for their bouquets. However, when New York City floral designer Elizabeth Ryan gets a request for a white bouquet, she takes it one step further. "I combine many different shades of white," says Ryan, "to make it more interesting. Also, I like to incorporate lots of texture and variety. I recently created a bouquet of white gardenias and black 'caviar' (viburnum) berries for a really striking look. Blue-green hydrangeas and eucalyptus pods are another pretty combination. And a bouquet of scented geraniums, roses, and marjoram—which looks and smells beautiful—makes a wonderful mix."

Large white casablanca lilies in a cascade bouquet or the summery blend of Hawaiian dendrobium orchids are choices that make a strong statement. For something a bit more traditional, you might combine white roses, stephanotis, and freesia. If you're set on using just a touch of color to catch the eye, try a pastel composition: pale peach Osiana roses, pink phlox, irises in the softest lavender, and champagne roses are a few favorites for achieving a romantic look.

Attendants' bouquets may be as colorful as you wish, and it's up to you whether the flowers you choose complement or contrast with the shade of their dresses. Do plan, though, to have the bouquets work with the rest of the wedding flowers, such as those used for centerpieces or the bows at the ends of church pews. Attention to these details will create unity and enhance the floral theme. For still more continuity, consider using the same type of flower in the attendants' bouquets as in the bride's bouquet. For instance, her creamy white roses may be complemented by roses in hot shades against deep velvet dresses or by roses in jewel tones with floral-print gowns.

❖ *Colorful blooms of pink astilbe, lavender sweet peas, dark pink roses, and blue delphiniums create a dramatic contrast with the pure white bridal dress. Photo by Iraida Icaza.*

To add a more personal touch to the bouquet, you might want to provide your florist with ribbon or pieces of fabric that match your wedding gown or attendants' dresses to be incorporated into the design. And if you want to toss your bouquet but don't really want to part with it, request that a simpler bouquet be made just for this event. Extra long ribbon streamers tied around the stems make for a fabulous photograph as the bouquet sails towards waiting hands.

∼ THE CEREMONY ∼

The flowers and colors you choose for your wedding ceremony will depend a great deal on the style of the church or temple, home or garden, or whatever site you have chosen. In a religious setting, your choices should be both joyful and dignified to convey the feeling of celebration. Consider the scale and architectural details of the building's interior when deciding on altar and pew decorations. For example, in a large space, don't make the mistake of spreading your dollars too thin. Instead of several small arrangements on the altar and bows on every pew, opt for a single grand altar composition and decorations for the first few family pews.

Many florists agree that the simple use of color plays an important role in flowers for the ceremony. A fresh, lively palette may be needed for contrast in a dark, wood-filled space, while a more modern, well-lit setting would benefit from a number of schemes ranging from rich, jewel tones to classic all-white. In fact, even less expensive white flowers, such as gladiolas, generally look regal at a ceremony when used in full, lush arrangements.

An increase in formal, traditional weddings is being noted by florists all over the country, and some of the charm of such ceremonies comes from the presence of fresh-faced—and unpredictable—children. Flower girls look absolutely delightful carrying bouquets and tossing rose petals.

More inventive contemporary designs have evolved for the youngest members of the wedding thanks to floral designers like David Kurio of Austin, Texas, who proposes, for example, that "if there are two children in the wedding, they can walk down the aisle each holding the end of a garland. That same garland can later be hung on the back of the bride's chair at the reception or across the guest-book table.

"In a Jewish ceremony, garlands can also be used to decorate the *huppah,* the canopy that symbolizes the couple's new home. Woven strands of lush flowers may trim the top edges and be entwined around the structure's poles. Another fresh idea is for flower girls to carry pomanders instead of bouquets. I've made them with stephanotis, roses, and alstromeria and hung them by wired French ribbon. If there are many children in the wedding, the girls could hold pomanders, and the boys could carry garlands."

❖ *An archway of greenery creates a handsome and intimate wedding bower within an oversized hotel ballroom. The pine boughs have been arranged to draw attention to the celebrants. The large pine cones convey a traditional meaning of good wishes for long life together. Flowers by Elizabeth Ryan. Photo by Z. Livnat.*

～ THE RECEPTION ～

*D*ecorating a reception site requires an eye for detail and an expert feel for color. Professional floral designers are able to transform your hall, club, or tent into precisely the space you envision—only lovelier.

Creativity has come to play an increasingly larger role at many wedding receptions. Happily, brides and grooms are contributing many more of their own ideas to help assemble a look that reflects their personalities. One Jewish wedding that took place in the fall, around the time of *Sukkot,* the festival of the harvest, included a variety of fruits and vegetables, such as peaches, lady apples, and cabbages, together with the flowers. The results were fabulous three-dimensional still-life paintings with an earthy scent.

Color is another consideration that greatly influences the overall look of your reception. Again, your florist should make recommendations to you based on the style and size of the space you've chosen. "My brides are a little older and more sophisticated now," says designer Ryan, "so they're paring down and going for funkier, wilder colors." To fill these requests, Ryan uses lots of jewel tones and flowers in vivid, rich shades such as butterscotch roses, purple anemones and burgundy dahlias, stock, and roses.

Ryan feels, too, that "lighting is everything" and likes to incorporate candles into her designs. "I also prefer to make each centerpiece a little—or very—different, and often add fruits and vegetables to the arrangements for a twist. Lemons are great in summer because their fragrance creates a nice atmosphere. In autumn, I like to bring in miniature vegetables, such as eggplants and squashes. And artichokes of any size—sometimes gilded—also look beautiful mixed in with flowers."

Creative florists strive for decorations with a difference. The unusual touches at a wedding are the most memorable, and designer Ryan welcomes the challenge to create such memories by improving upon standard floral ideas.

❖ The colors and scents of rich jewel-toned flowers mixed with fresh fruits makes a sophisticated, heady arrangement. Leaf-edged votives encircle the creation for added drama. Flowers by Elizabeth Ryan. Photo by Z. Livnat.

Garlands, those fragrant lengths of flowers and greenery that accent a ceremony in so many wonderful ways, may also enhance the points of interest at your reception. As the covering for a mantel, the valance atop a window, or the decoration surrounding a cake, garlands highlight areas that might otherwise go unnoticed, while helping to shape a more romantic environment. An ideal spot for a garland is around a banister. Other staircase decorations might include a full length of baby's breath and a bouquet at the bottom with an ivy trail, or boughs of holly for a holiday wedding. While visiting the site you've chosen, your floral designer may notice other suitable spots for flowers, so be sure to ask for his or her ideas.

From delicate to dramatic, floral arrangements can add an enchanting element to your wedding, surrounding you with warmth, beauty, and romance.

❖ (Opposite) Left: Brilliant roses, lilies, and succulent berries create a dramatic reception table centerpiece for a winter holiday wedding. Right: Holiday-inspired place settings and a gold star tree ornament favor for each guest highlighted this grand reception. Photos by George Otero.

❖ (Right) Whether bound in a bouquet or adorning a wedding site, flowers enhance the wedding theme. During the holidays, a lush Della Robbia garland of fruits and greenery looks festive lining a banister—a suitable stage from which the bride can toss her bouquet. Flowers: Castle & Pierpont. Photo by Bernard Vidal.

❖ *(Above)* *Five little flower girls, all dressed in white, each wear a wreath and carry a nosegay of roses mixed with greenery. Photo by Barber Photography.*

❖ *(Above, right)* *The charm and innocence of little girls: Wearing halos of soft-colored roses, these flower girls gather round for last-minute instructions. Photo by Maureen De Fries for Laurie Klein Studio.*

❖ *(Opposite)* *One pretty flower girl peeks outs from behind the bride's gown. On her head, a sweet wreath of roses and other dainty blooms. Photo by Iraida Icaza.*

THE RECEPTION

*Y*our wedding reception celebrates your marriage, pampers your guests, and marks the glorious culmination of months of planning. The tone of the party will be largely determined by your own personal style as well as the location site and what you serve. The possibilities are exciting and varied, and sometimes the sky is the limit.

～ SITES ～

*I*n recent years, traditional wedding plans have been altered to fit more contemporary needs. On average, brides and grooms are now several years older and generally more sophisticated than their counterparts of fifty years ago. Although it has been customary for the bride's family to host the reception, many dual-career couples now pay for all or part of their wedding celebration.

These changes in lifestyles and personal tastes go hand in hand with the refreshing trend toward less traditional wedding sites. The recent roster of new and interesting wedding locales includes yachts, gardens, mansions, museums and art galleries, zoos, fairgrounds, bed-and-breakfast inns, movie studio lots, wineries—and, of course, the fantasy capital of the country, Disney World.

❖ *(Previous spread) A festive reception table set with many trumpet-shaped vases of loosely arranged gypsophilia and miniature carnations provides lyric contrast with the room's dark draperies and lamp shades while echoing the natural landscape outside the window. Photo by Elizabeth Heyert.*

❖ *(Opposite) The view from behind a traditional dais shows off the details: The bride and groom's chairs are bedecked with fresh flowers—and the wait staff stands at the ready. Photo by Barber Photography.*

❖ *(Right) Majestic mirrors reflect the light in a stately mansion with remarkable detailing. Photo by Ronald J. Krowne. Courtesy of Culinary Architect Catering.*

Whatever site you are considering, it's a good idea to visit—if at all possible, when another wedding is taking place there. While there, request a sample meal from the caterer, take a tour of the kitchen, and inspect the restrooms; a careful look at all the facilities is essential to hosting a happy and trouble-free party yourselves.

Having a wedding at home—yours or your parents' or a friend's—is another wonderful option, providing there is ample space. Marrying in a place that holds many special memories can be a pleasurable alternative to a rental site. Although the romance of this idea may seem irresistible, there are many factors to contemplate before you commit to it. First, consider that it's likely that your home won't have the parking spaces, restroom facilities, or electrical capabilities needed to accommodate a large crowd. And providing these may prove to be a costly and logistical problem. Hiring your own caterer and decorator to furnish a site may be the choice of many who are prepared to pay, but this prospect can be surprisingly complicated. Careful planning—and perhaps the services of a wedding coordinator—are recommended for those whose hearts are set on an at-home reception.

As wedding fêtes grow grander and guest lists grow longer, more and more brides and grooms are turning to hotels with spacious accommodations. When you book a hotel reception, the essential services are already in place. In addition to a chef, of course, a staff florist and bridal coordinator are usually available to you. Out-of-town guests may also reserve

rooms in the hotel, usually at special rates. And some even offer their bridal suite to newlyweds for the wedding night as part of an arranged package. Even if the hotel you select for your reception offers all these services, you are not necessarily compelled to use them. If you have a favorite florist and caterer, it may be possible to hire them instead. Speak with the hotel representative about your preferences.

❖ *A holiday-time reception just spills over with design possibilities. Making a grand impression here, a Christmas tree with twinkling lights, a wreath dressed with golden bows and velvet fruits, and a mantel draped with greenery, pomegranates, and pine cones. Flowers: Castle & Pierpont. Photo by Jeremy Samuelson.*

~ FOOD ~

exans love a barbecue, New Yorkers savor the sit-down dinner. In between, the menu options are endless. An hors d'ouevres buffet, beach clambake, dessert reception, champagne brunch, cocktail dinner buffet, afternoon tea, or garden luncheon have all served as appropriate wedding parties.

Regardless of the format you choose, beautiful tables and an elegant menu seem to result almost effortlessly when an experienced caterer unleashes his or her talents and love of good food. Spring and summer receptions can benefit

❖ *A table of fabulous-looking vegetable tarts is ready to serve at a buffet reception. Food by Creative Edge Parties. Photo by Alex Kirkbride.*

from the bounty of the freshest produce and flavors of the season. For fall and winter, heartier fare that warms and comforts makes a fitting menu. And, of course, almost anything you want can be obtained at any time of year—if you are willing to pay for it.

An open exchange of menu ideas with your caterer is very important: discuss everything from hors d'ouevres to desserts. Share your preferences, and learn about his or her favorite seasonal choices and signature recipes. Talk about your tastes and ethnic backgrounds in order to tailor a more personalized event through the food you serve. Also, be sure to ask the caterer to visit your reception site since many of today's more unique locations may not have all the kitchen facilities necessary to prepare certain menus.

Consider the elements of the bar as well, and what constitutes an appropriate amount and type of liquor for your reception. The right number of champagne bottles should be ready to pour, and complementary dinner wines served at the proper times. A good caterer will also know how much liquor will be needed according to changes in the seasons (more Scotch is drunk in winter months, and vodka or gin in the summer, for example).

The ability to fulfill challenging wishes is another sign of a capable caterer. For many couples, weddings offer an opportunity to display pride in their heritages, and the menu serves as a mirror to their ethnic origins. A meal including an eclectic blend of international foods is a common request heard by many caterers. Carla Ruben and Chef Robert Spiegel, owners of

Creative Edge Parties, a New York City catering firm, have coordinated and cooked for an endless variety of just such weddings.

For the marriage of a Greek groom and his Korean bride, Ruben and Spiegel created a diverse menu of foods representing their homelands. This casual, fun, and light menu featured hors d'oeuvres of eggplant moussaka squares and chick pea cakes with feta cheese compote right alongside crunchy mung bean pancakes filled with diced ham and scallions, and grilled shrimp marinated in lemons and celery leaf.

A Moroccan feast catered by Creative Edge Parties was enhanced by decorative details. "The party was held under an authentic Moroccan tent," says Ruben, "and pillows were placed on the chairs. They added beautiful color to the space." The menu centered around rolled flatbread filled with lamb and dates; tangine of red snapper with prunes and saffron; a salad of couscous, fava beans, haricots verts, and mint; Moroccan breads with roasted eggplant dip; a "coiled" serpent cake with almond filling and peaches in rosewater with mint and cinnamon for dessert—and much more.

A classic antipasto table helped kicked off a traditional Italian sit-down dinner that ended with wedding cake, crème brûlé napoleon, biscotti, and

❖ *(Top) Food presentation is every bit as important as taste. Dessert makes for a very sweet ending, especially when it is one as beautiful—and delicious—as this baked pear tart by Creative Edge Parties. Photo by Falk Langner.*

❖ *(Left) The art of presentation is carried to a high level with this handsome way to present an icy display of seafood. Photo by Iceculture, Inc.*

cappuccino. In between, guests were treated to four courses, from a trio of pastas and seafood terrine to roast loin of veal and baked figs with cambozola cheese.

A cup of cheer—without the alcohol—is an increasingly welcome addition to many wedding celebrations. More health-conscious guests are consuming less alcohol these days, making it necessary to offer other thirst-quenching options.

One such alternative is a water bar, stocked with the wet stuff in all its newest forms. Include the sparkling, mineral, fruit-flavored, and spring varieties. Add seltzer, club soda, and tonic water for extra fizz. Sparkling Water Distributors in Long Island City, New York, will even supply water in bottles with personalized wedding labels.

Besides water, beverage requests include sparkling cider (a suitable champagne stand-in for toasting) and other bubbly fruit juices. Today, it's also quite acceptable to serve frozen blender drinks without the alcohol. Margaritas still have zing sans tequila, and piña coladas taste tropical even without the rum.

Cool, colorful punch is another wonderful alternative to the usual assortment of reception drinks. Fresh and fruity, punch recipes are especially perfect for summer weddings and bridal showers.

There is also a compromise for those who prefer something stronger than water, but lighter than hard liquor. A white bar offers wine, champagne, and mixed vodka, gin, and rum drinks. For afternoon or brunch receptions, you might offer guests crystal cups of champagne punch during the cocktail hour. It's an elegant—and economical—change from an open bar.

❖ *Seasonal reds and greens draw attention to the handsome fireplace that serves as the perfect backdrop for the punch table. Flowers by Castle & Pierpont. Photo by Jeremy Samuelson.*

∼ DECOR ∼

A reception room is basically a blank stage waiting to be transformed by flowers, lighting, and props. Many brides choose to take on the task themselves, others leave it to a floral designer or wedding consultant. Remember that whoever decorates the space should possess an eye for detail and a rich imagination.

Keep in mind that some locations may cry out for a specific theme, while others require more work and inspiration. Thanks to the amazing variety of party goods that can be rented, everything from linens and lights to gazebos and greenery are available to bring an image to life. Wedding consultants will help you to plan almost any size reception, performing a varying list of duties. And those professionals who oversee the event from start to finish are generally capable of working magic with any given decor.

In one elegantly lavish Miami wedding, planning was taken to new heights. Exquisite globe topiaries of orchids, roses, and wonderfully performed freesia—all in white, and each ringed with oil lamps—were suspended from the ceiling over each table. This is certainly a creative and glamorous way to guarantee that conversation with one's tablemates is not inhibited by towering centerpieces.

At June Wedding, Inc., in San Francisco, Robbi Ernst oversees all, with a bit of guidance from the bride and groom. "When I look at a bare room, I first consider

❖ *Suspended in air: Exquisite globe topiaries of white orchids, roses, and wonderfully perfumed freesia, ringed with oil lamp globes, hang from the ceiling. Clusters of pillar candles interspersed with the same blooms on the navy moiré-covered table tops echo the light and fragrance from above. Regulation gold hotel ballroom chairs are swathed in white and navy moiré silk. Flowers by Josh Behar. Photo by Greg Hark.*

decorating the walls, then work inward," says Ernst, who gives clients a monthly computer readout of their checklist. "Ideas start to fall into place once the theme takes over, but there are certain rules that always apply. Lighting is the first, since it adds a dimension like nothing else can. Linens are another: you must have cloths down to the floor and use overlays for depth."

A reception at San Francisco's Academy of Sciences in Golden Gate Park required careful planning. During cocktails in the aquarium, sushi was served on silver trays. A sit-down dinner followed in the African room of the Natural History Museum. Against the backdrop of elegant architecture and exotic animals, zebra-patterned tablecloths and leafy palms turned one exhibit hall into a wondrous safari setting. And the event ran like clockwork with Ernst at the helm. The choreography of the evening was planned out in exacting detail.

And what would you expect when two people in the party planning business marry each other? Unforgettable results—and a windfall of great ideas. That's precisely what came with the lavish wedding of a party planner and the owner of a party tent rental business who devised a scheme using the four seasons.

❖ *(Opposite) An appealing tent on a beautifully manicured lawn is an irresistible setting for a summer late afternoon-into-evening reception. Photo by Barber Photography.*

❖ *(Above) A great locale can be the perfect springboard for a wedding theme. For a reception held in the Natural History Museum at San Francisco's Academy of Sciences, a safari setting was inspired by the animals on display in the African room. Decor by June Weddings, Inc. Photo by Post Street Portraits.*

❖ *(Right) A papier-mache swan, brimming over with fresh flowers, is set amidst the placecards to help welcome wedding guests. Flowers and photo by Lamsback Floral Decorators.*

❖ *The ceremony tent was draped with yards of white fabric and illuminated with richly colored lights. Photo by Sarah Merians.*

❖ *"Spring," the centerpiece of the reception room, featured floral tablecloths and matching chair bows. Photo by Sarah Merians.*

After the ceremony in one beautiful tent, guests were led to a reception room filled with tents and awnings used to define the areas for the seasons. Guests entered the room through "fall," a rustic scene complete with rugs, tapestries, velvet tablecloths, and log furniture.

"Spring," the centerpiece of the entire room, featured a tree trunk dressed up with magnolia branches and surrounded by wrought-iron garden furniture. The dance floor was hand painted to match the pattern of the tablecloths, a floral done in sherbet shades of apricot, celadon, and lavender. Ivory chair covers were tied with matching floral bows.

A front porch was created for a "summer" mood with a huge photographic mural of woods and a yard as backdrop. The umbrellas topping the tables were hand painted with flowers to match the cloths. Wicker furniture, including a great wicker bar, and a black-and-white striped awning anchored the whole summery spot.

❖ *The rustic, autumnal setting for "fall" centered on rugs, log furniture, and colorful leaves. Photo by Sarah Merians.*

❖ *A completely white winter wonderland area, right down to the light. Photo by Sarah Merians.*

Billowing fabric, strung with thousands of twinkle lights from behind, formed a ceiling awning for the "winter" wonderland. This season was dressed all in white, from the satin tablecloths to the ballroom chairs covered in organza. For these tables, Party Artistry, the bride's company, created unique centerpieces of light box platforms topped with bubble vases filled with casablanca lilies submerged in water.

The dinner was a "grazing" format without assigned seating. Each section had its seasonal buffet table. Of course, flowers played a tremendous role in the entire theme. The four corners of the dance floor in "spring" had "flower towers"—room pillars covered from floor to ceiling with blooms and greenery. And low hedges and topiaries camouflaged the band's equipment and defined the bandstand area.

After the cake cutting came the finishing touch. The tent walls behind "summer" and "winter" were parted to reveal another room complete with a roulette wheel, black-jack tables, and slot machines for a fabulous mini casino.

❖ *Limos by land, but boat by sea: This bride and groom conveniently docked right at their waterside reception site. Photo by Maripat Goodwin Photography.*

❖ *These richly set tables, lit by dozens of candles in many sizes, followed the curves of the splendid porch at The Octagon House in Irvington-on-Hudson, New York. Photo by Andrew French.*

❖ *(Opposite) A vast stone patio with a center fountain made the perfect place to mingle at this outdoor reception. (Above and right) A casually chic wedding reception on the beach at Malibu, complete with shoeless guests and celebrants— and a place to park footwear. Photos by Barber Photography.*

THE CAKE

The tradition of the wedding cake began in ancient Rome. As an offering to Jupiter, the groom tasted the barley or wheat cake, then broke it over the head of the bride; guests shared the fallen crumbs. In the Middle Ages, newlyweds kissed over a stack of sweetened buns. When a French pastry chef iced one such stack, the modern wedding cake was born.

Although this confection has gone through many transformations along the way, the ritual of cutting the cake is still an important one, steeped in meaning. Sharing a champagne toast and the tradition of watching the bride and groom feed each other a sweet sample of cake are highlights of any wedding celebration. Therefore, the baker you choose must understand the vision you have of this special cake.

When you interview bakers, ask a series of questions. For instance, can the baker reproduce the style of a cake you spotted in a book or magazine—but in very different flavors? If you choose a design from a personal portfolio, will the baker alter an aspect of the decoration or recipe for you? Is the baker experienced at creating custom-designed cakes or unique shapes? Are only natural ingredients used? How soon before your celebration will the cake be baked? Finally, take a taste test: once you've come close to a decision, ask to try a smaller sample cake before making your final choice.

❖ *(Previous spread) A moment worth waiting for—the cutting of the cake. The bride and groom and their guests enjoy this part of the wedding ritual as much as any. The attractive confection was created by Albert Kumin. Photo by Bill Margerin.*

❖ *(Opposite) This magnificent cake features a crown topper, monogram of the newlyweds' initials, and rolled-back leaves embossed with an imprint of the bride's lace. Cake by Ron Ben-Israel. Photo by Edward Addeo.*

❖ *(Right) Fruity garlands and wreaths, rich gold braids and bows—all the signs of the season adorn the festive holiday wedding cake by Colette Peters. Photo by Bernard Vidal.*

～ CAKE DESIGNS ～

*T*oday's wedding cakes come from the kitchens of some very talented bakers and are triumphs of both design and taste. They may display artful details or whimsical touches, petals made of frosting and shaped into perfect flowers, and sweet cake layers filled with fresh cremes or fruit. Some cakes are circled with designs as delicate as those on a bridal gown. Others are trimmed in motifs that echo the reception's decor. In any design, a cake is a treasured memory for the bride and groom.

Cakes have become increasingly important elements in today's more opulent weddings. Bakers now set out to make edible works of art to please more sophisticated tastes. Once you have determined the style of your wedding cake, discuss with your baker the many decorations, fillings, and flavors that he or she is able to create.

No longer content with the usual recipes, newlyweds want cakes that make a statement—inside and out. Spicy carrot, tangy lemon creme, and mocha mousse are among the many options offered by expressive bakers.

Ellen Baumwoll, an award-winning baker and owner of Bijoux Doux ("Sweet Jewels") Specialty Cakes in New York City, notes that "the majority of couples I work with choose chocolate cake or a rich chocolate truffle filling. Another popular request is for a hazelnut/almond cake I often make for weddings—but with a chocolate filling!"

The way to please a wide variety of tastes is by asking that each tier be a different flavor—then there's sure to be something for everyone.

❖ *(Left) This square, single layer cake by James E. Kennedy is festooned with lacework and a sugary gardenia—perfect for a small reception or bridal shower. Photo by John W. Corbett.*

❖ *(Opposite) A tribute to autumn, this colorful cake by Mark Barrie Tasker is decorated with the symbols of a harvest. Handmade marzipan fruits tumble out of the cornucopia topper and onto the tiers below. Photo by Martin Jacobs.*

To complement the luscious inside, nothing less than pulled sugar ribbons, gold icing, or an intricate cake top will do to adorn the outside of your cake. Surface decoration can take on many looks: piping, lettering, ribbons, chocolate curls, trelliswork, and hand-rolled roses can create an individualized look. And sugar can be shaped into the most marvelous things: lacy edges, tiny marzipan fruits, a garden of flowers.

Cile Bellefleur-Burbidge, widely recognized as a leader in the art of cake decorating, captures a Victorian style in her creations that are a marvel to behold. From her home's kitchen in Danvers, Massachusetts, she turns out towering cakes that are

❖ *Every inch of the exquisite floral arches on this ethereal cake— including each wispy "ribbon"— is edible and completely made by hand. Cake by Ron Ben-Israel. Photo by Guy Powers.*

covered with her signature touches. "I use many scrolls, fences, floral arrangements, and latticework as decoration. Everything is created by piping royal icing onto a buttercream frosting. And edible gold leaf is now a popular accent that I've also used many times."

For a very different look, a rolled fondant icing is the preferred topping for many bakers because its smooth finish is easy to decorate or quilt with the proper tools.

"I only use rolled English fondant on my cakes," says Ron Ben-Israel, who turns out incredible confections from his New York City kitchen. "Fondant doesn't shine like buttercream, so you get a smooth, matte finish with soft, rounded edges, which I think is very bridal. It has the same consistency as marzipan but is made without nuts so you can get a pure white color or add elements that change the color to create very pale shades using coffee for ivories, pistachios for a hint of green and raspberries for a beautiful 'rum pink.' Best of all, fondant is fat free."

Ben-Israel adorns his cakes with his own "sugarwork" flowers, ribbons, and bows, artfully shaped of the sweet stuff and made to last a very long time. "My inspiration for these ornaments comes from nature, fashions, and fabrics," says the designer. "I often make a mold of a lace swatch from a bride's gown and use it to imprint my sugar ribbons and bows so the cake coordinates with the gown. I also provide monogrammed boxes for the couple so they can have their sugar flowers as keepsakes. Many place them on mantels and Christmas trees through the years."

Beneath the icing, Ben-Israel tempts the palate with incredible flavor combinations. Imported Swiss meringue buttercream (the lightest and fluffiest you'll find) is turned into chocolate, cappuccino, praline, or vanilla fillings and teamed with layers of luscious cake, usually moistened with a liqueur.

❖ *The subtly colored cascade of sugar flowers and sweet, satiny ribbons on this five-tiered cake by Ron Ben-Israel looks incredibly realistic. The topper can be saved indefinitely for a wonderful keepsake. Photo by Guy Powers.*

❖ *(Above) Delicate handmade flowers are scattered atop a one-tier cake iced in rolled fondant. Cake by Cheryl Kleinman Cakes. Photo by Tony Cenicola.*
❖ *(Right) Shades of white provide a subtle and elegant contrast on this piped dome confection from Cheryl Kleinman Cakes. Photo by Tony Cenicola.*

"My most requested cake is chocolate with Kahlua, Amaretto, or Grand Marnier, my favorite," says Ben-Israel, who strives to combine flavor with aesthetics. "A cake must also look great," he says, "so I always create a beautiful exterior or try to recreate a couple's dream." For one bride and groom who met and fell in love in Manhattan, Ben-Israel shaped the city's skyline in tempered white and dark chocolate, and wove it around the cake. Symbols of their courtship — Shea Stadium, restaurants, Radio City Music Hall — stood out in the design. For a millinery artist, he shaped a tiered cake of hat boxes and gift boxes done in white and dark chocolate. "And as a finishing touch," says Ben-Israel, "the couple requested teddy bears on top."

A fine arts background has also steered the hand of Margaret Braun, another New York City cake designer who brings beauty to her craft. "I look at art through the ages — especially the Renaissance and Medieval periods — and try to translate it into cakes," says Braun, who rarely uses flowers, sugar or otherwise. "I like to work with color and silver and gold leaf. My base is usually fondant topped with lots of intricate, detailed piping done with royal icing."

Topping Braun's most-favored list is a chocolate cake filled with hazelnut ganache and a trace of apricot preserves. Another sweet suggestion: buttery pound cake, dense and moist, filled with a fresh, strong contrast such as a raspberry framboise. "However, if the wedding cake is the only dessert," says Braun, "I recommend chocolate. If there's something served in addition, a citrus flavored cake is often a nice accompaniment." For baker Baumwoll, fondant is actually a necessity when she's working one of her favorite styles of confections. "I design an Americanized version of the Australian cake, which is characterized by a smooth surface with beveled edges and lots of fine decorations. The intricate lace and embroidery work is done with an extremely tiny tube—the results actually resemble fabric. Fondant or similar icings, such as rolled white chocolate or marzipan, must be used to create the effect."

For many bakers, the wedding itself is the richest source of decorating ideas. Cheryl Kleinman, who operates Cheryl Kleinman Cakes in New York City, likes the cake to echo elements of the wedding. "The theme or color scheme should somehow be matched in the cake. It's a very personal point, and I work with them to create exactly what they envision, since everyone has different ideas. In fact, the only thing many of my clients now commonly request is that their cakes have a strong, bold design that can be seen from across the room."

❖ *Edible silver-leaf diamonds and dragees glisten among the icy shades of blue and white on this masterfully designed "sweet" by Margaret Braun. A perfect choice for a New Year's wedding. Photo by Martin Jacobs.*

~ CAKE TOPS ~

A miniature marvel, the top of your cake will have a big impact on the overall finished look, so choose a style that sweetly complements the cake's basic design. Flowers, both fresh-cut and sugar dough, are beautiful additions. Traditional tops, such as a bride and groom,

are still making appearances on towering treats, but today most wedding cakes are designed without them.

Many of today's bakers bring an artistic background to their work and can design spectacular tops. Cile Bellefleur-Burbidge has seen a rise in the request for miniature gazebos. Cheryl Kleinman sculpted a Hawaiian island, complete with a couple atop a volcano. Ellen Baumwoll created a replica of the Sacred Heart Church in Prague for one architect-groom who greatly admired that building. She also once shaped an airplane from sugar paste for a couple who met in flight. And the Roman Colosseum was requested by another groom whose fiancée was of Italian heritage. (*He* provided a small pair of lions, one wearing a wedding veil, the other wearing a tie!)

Bakers can accommodate almost any request. The right tools and a practiced hand can turn any idea into reality.

A unique cake top also serves as a keepsake, since many newlyweds still follow the tradition of freezing the top layer of their cake and eating it on their first wedding anniversary. Those who have carefully preserved the confection can enjoy an evening—and a dessert—filled with sweet memories.

～ THE CAKE TABLE ～

The wedding reception culminates in the cutting of a fabulous cake, designed just for you for this day. Anything that treats your senses of smell, sight, and taste to such a wonderful lift deserves a showcase of its own. Thus, once you have commissioned your ideal wedding cake, plan to display it on a suitably designed cake table. Many couples choose to

❖ *(Opposite) A Phillipine wedding featured an elaborate structure of 12 cakes topped with sugary flowers and "draped" icing swags. Photo by Barber Photography.*

❖ *(Right) A marvelously witty approach to the fine art of wedding cakes—a towering confection representing the bride and groom's favorite books—paperbacks on the side! Cake by Anna Paz. Photo by Greg Hark.*

have the cake on display throughout the reception; others have the table brought into the room after the meal, signaling the end of the festivities. Either way, this detail requires special attention.

Keeping in mind that your cake is the centerpiece, concentrate on adding elements that enhance its design. Display an elegant cake knife and server set in cut crystal or sterling silver and tied with rich ribbons; a beautiful tablecloth; the bride's bouquet; and perhaps a grouping of slender champagne flutes.

～ THE GROOM'S CAKE ～

*B*efore the introduction of powdery white flour and leavening in eighteenth-century America, the wedding cake was traditionally a dense, rich fruitcake. Today, the "groom's cake" carries on this custom, although chocolate has replaced fruit in popularity.

Generally just one layer, this confection is often baked in a shape or topped with a design that depicts the groom's interests or hobbies. The cake is cut and served at the reception or distributed in individual boxes to departing guests. A single woman who places a sliver of the cake under her pillow that night will supposedly dream of her future husband.

Extraordinary details that only a practiced hand can produce.

❖ *(Opposite) Royal icing lacework and elaborate scrolls blanket the tiers of this magnificent confection by Albert Kumin. Miniature marzipan fruits, white chocolate angels, and the pulled sugar basket topper are astounding in their detail. Photo by Bill Margerin.*

❖ *(Right) A groom's cake for the chess-loving groom, in white and dark chocolate. Cake by Anna Paz. Photo by Greg Hark.*

~ Sources ~

Photographers

EDWARD ADDEO
214 West 29th St.
New York, NY 10001

JON BARBER
Barber Photography
34071 LaPlaza
Suite 100
Dana Point, CA 92629

JOHN M. CERRITELLI
Prestige-Barkley
190 Ferry Blvd.
Stratford, CT 06497

TONY CENICOLA
325 West 37th St.
New York, NY 10018

MARY COONEY
Pamela Benepe Photography
55 Valley Rd.
Easton, CT 06612

SIDNEY COOPER
1427 East Fourth St.
Studio 2
Los Angeles, CA 90033

JOHN W. CORBETT
928 West Main Rd.
Middletown, RI 02840

GREY CRAWFORD
1714 Lyndon St.
South Pasadena, CA 91031

MAUREEN EDWARDS DEFRIES
P.O. Box 749
Hawleyville, CT 06440

ROBBI ERNST
June Weddings, Inc.
325 Roosevelt Way
San Francisco, CA 91364

RICHARD FANNING
Richard Fanning Photography
7 Whitney St.
Westport, CT 06880

MARILI FORASTIERI
Contact: Judy Casey
212-255-3252

ANDREW FRENCH
698 West End Ave.
New York, NY 10025

TIM GEANY
Contact: Yellen Lashapelle
212-838-3170

MARIPAT GOODWIN PHOTOGRAPHER
57 Old Highway
Southbury, CT 06488

GREG HARK PHOTOGRAPHICS
327 West 47th St.
Miami Beach, FL 33140

DAVID HECHLER
Harold Hechler Associates, Ltd.
67 Gladstone Rd.
New Rochelle, NY 19804

ELIZABETH HEYERT
666 Greenwich St.
New York, NY 10014

PETER HÖGG
1221 South La Brea
Los Angeles, CA 90019

IRAIDA ICAZA
51 White St.
New York, NY 10013

MARTIN JACOBS
59 West 19th St., Room 2A
New York, NY 10011

PHYLLIS KEENAN PHOTOGRAPHY
29 William St.
Danbury, CT 06810

ALEX KIRKBRIDE
21 East 9th St.
New York, NY 10003

LAURIE KLEIN
Laurie Klein Gallery
20 Station Rd.
Brookfield, CT 06804

Z. LIVNAT
411 East 9th St.
New York, NY 10009

BILL MARGERIN
41 West 25th St.
8th Floor
New York, NY 10010

SARAH MERIANS
101 Fifth Ave., 5th Floor
New York, NY 10003

CHRISTINE NEWMAN
Persona Grata Photography
107 Sixth St.
Hoboken, NJ 07030

GEORGE OTERO
115 West 23rd St.
New York, NY 10011

GUY POWERS
130 West 25th St.
4th Floor
New York, NY 10001

JEREMY SAMUELSON
1188 South La Brea
Los Angeles, CA 90019

GEORGIA SHERON
Georgia Sheron Photography
228 Main St.
Oakville, CT 06779

BERNARD VIDAL
Contact: Alice Morales
212-255-3252

Wedding Dresses

AMSALE ABERRA, INC.
347 West 39th St.
New York, NY 10018

CAROLINA HERRERA, LTD.
501 Seventh Ave.
New York, NY 10018

CHANEL
5 East 57th St.
New York, NY 10022

CHRISTIAN DIOR
499 Seventh Ave.
New York, NY 10018

DOLCE & GABBANA
532 Broadway
New York, NY 10012

JESSICA MCCLINTOCK
1412 Broadway
New York, NY 10018

JIM HJELM INTERNATIONAL LTD.
501 Seventh Ave.
New York, NY 10018

LAURA ASHLEY, INC.
714 Madison Ave.
New York, NY 10021

LILI
1117 East Main St.
Alhambra, CA 91801

MICHELE PICCIONE FOR ALFRED ANGELO
116 Welsh Rd.
Horsham, PA 19044

PRISCILLA OF BOSTON
40 Chambers St.
Charlestown, MA 02129

SUSAN LANE'S COUNTRY ELEGANCE
7353 Greenbush Ave.
North Hollywood, CA 91605

ULLA-MAJA
805 Madison Ave.
New York, NY 10022

VAN LEAR BRIDALS, INC.
1375 Broadway
New York, NY 10018

MICHELE VINCENT/ALFRED ANGELO
791 Park of Commerce Blvd.
Boca Raton, FL 33487

VERA WANG BRIDAL COLLECTION
25 East 77th St.
New York, NY 10021

Accessories

CAROLINA AMATO ACCESSORIES
389 Fifth Ave.
New York, NY 10016

CHICAGO BEAD WORKS
1998 Imio St.
Lisle, IL 60532

CHRISTIAN DIOR JEWELRY
417 Fifth Ave.
New York, NY 10016

LA CRASIA GLOVES, INC.
304 Fifth Ave.
New York, NY 10001

PETER FOX SHOES
105 Thompson St.
New York, NY 10012
712 Montana Ave.
Santa Monica, CA 90403

REEM ACRA BRIDALS
Gloves
10 Waterside Plaza
New York, NY 10010

TIA MAZZA MILLINERY
430 East 86th St.
New York, NY 10028

STUART WIETZMAN & CO.
Shoes
50 West 57th St.
New York, NY 10019

T & G BRIDAL VEILS
1375 Broadway
New York, NY 10018

Caterers

CREATIVE EDGE PARTIES
The Archive Building
110 Barrow St.
New York, NY 10014

CULINARY ARCHITECTS, INC.
475 Port Washington Blvd.
Port Washington, NY 11050

GLORIOUS FOOD
504 East 74th St.
New York, NY 10021

MOVABLE FEAST
284 Prospect Park West
Brooklyn, NY 11215

Wedding Cakes

ELLEN BAUMWOLL
Bijoux Doux Specialty Cakes and
    Pastries
304 Mulberry St.
New York, NY 10012

CILE BELLEFLEUR-BURBIDGE
12 Stafford Rd.
Danvers, MA 01923

RON BEN-ISRAEL CAKES
130 West 35th St.
New York, NY 10001

MARGARET BRAUN
33 Bank St.
New York, NY 10014

JAMES E. KENNEDY, JR., CONFECTIONS
231 New Boston Rd.
Fall River, MA 02720

CHERYL KLEINMAN
448 Atlantic Ave.
Brooklyn, NY 11217

KEVIN PAVLINA
P.O. Box 246
Northville, MI 48167

ANNA PAZ
1460 N.W. 107th Ave.
Unit B
Miami, FL 33172

COLETTE PETERS
327 West 11th St.
New York, NY 10014

SYLVIA WEINSTOCK
273 Church St.
New York, NY 10014

Ice Sculptures

ICECULTURE, INC.
P.O. Box 232
Hensall, Ontario
Canada

Floral Designers

ALL ABOUT FLOWERS—
    KAREN BRADLEY BARLETTA
420 Mountain St.
Cheshire, CT 06410

JOSH BEHAR
Atlas Floral
1060 Holland Dr.
Boca Raton, FL 33487

PAUL BOTT BEAUTIFUL FLOWERS
1305 Madison Ave.
New York, NY 10014

CASTLE & PIERPONT
1441 York Ave.
New York, NY 10021

STACY DANIELS
807 Washington St. #2
New York, NY 10014

ANCEL FABRICE
225 East 76th St.
New York, NY 10021

DAVID KURIO FLORIST
1201B West 6th St.
Austin, TX 78703

DIANE JAMISON—PERSONAL FLOWERS
4 South Pinehurst Ave.
New York, NY 10033

LAMSBACK FLORAL DECORATORS
148 Vine St.
Philadelphia, PA 19106

OPPIZZI & COMPANY
818 Greenwich Ave.
New York, NY 10014

ANDREW PASCOE
221 South St.
Oyster Bay, NY 11771

RENNY
159 East 64th St.
New York, NY 10021

ELIZABETH RYAN
411 East 9th St.
New York, NY 10009

WILDFLOWER
101 New Dorp Plaza
Staten Island, NY 10306

Wedding Consultants

A WEDDING MADE IN PARADISE
P.O. Box 986
Kihei
Maui, Hawaii 96753
1-800-453-3440

FANTASIA
St. Thomas, US Virgin Islands
1-800-FANTASIA

JUNE WEDDINGS, INC.
325 Roosevelt Way
San Francisco, CA 91364

WINE COUNTRY WEDDINGS
P.O. Box 13
Oakville, CA 94562

~ INDEX ~